AF469380

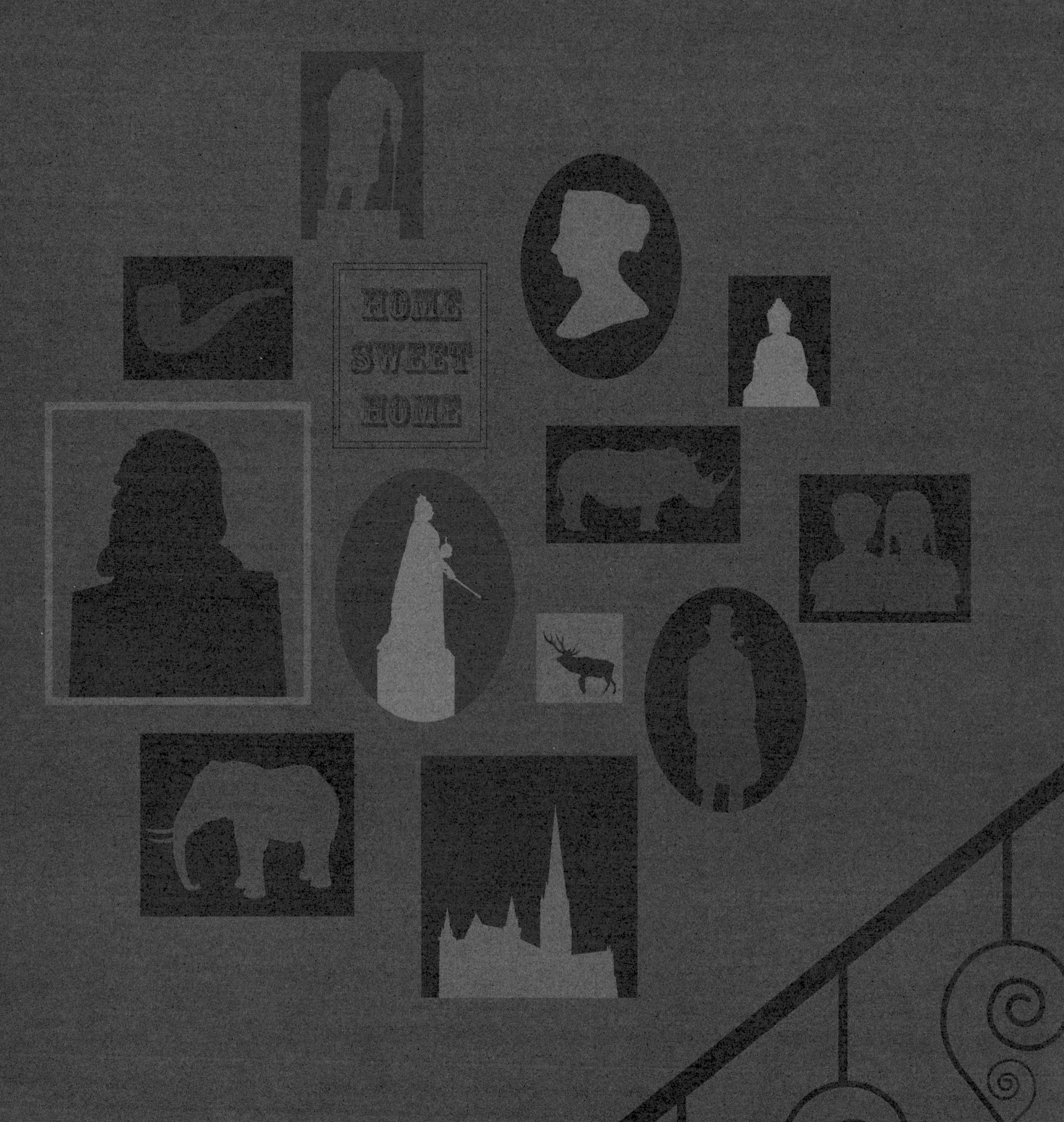
HOME
SWEET
HOME

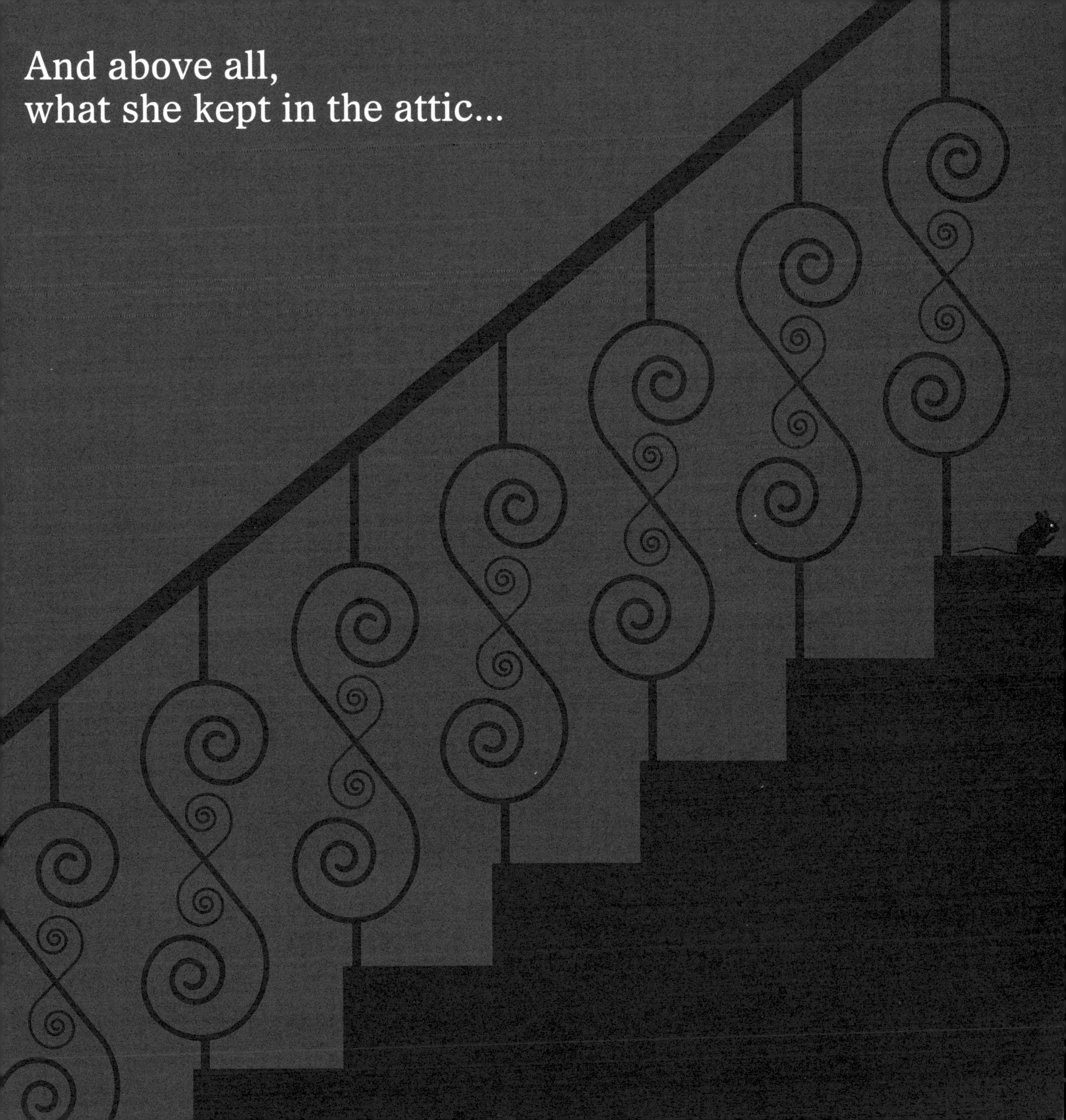
And above all,
what she kept in the attic...

I secretly hoped she'd
leave me the cuckoo clock...

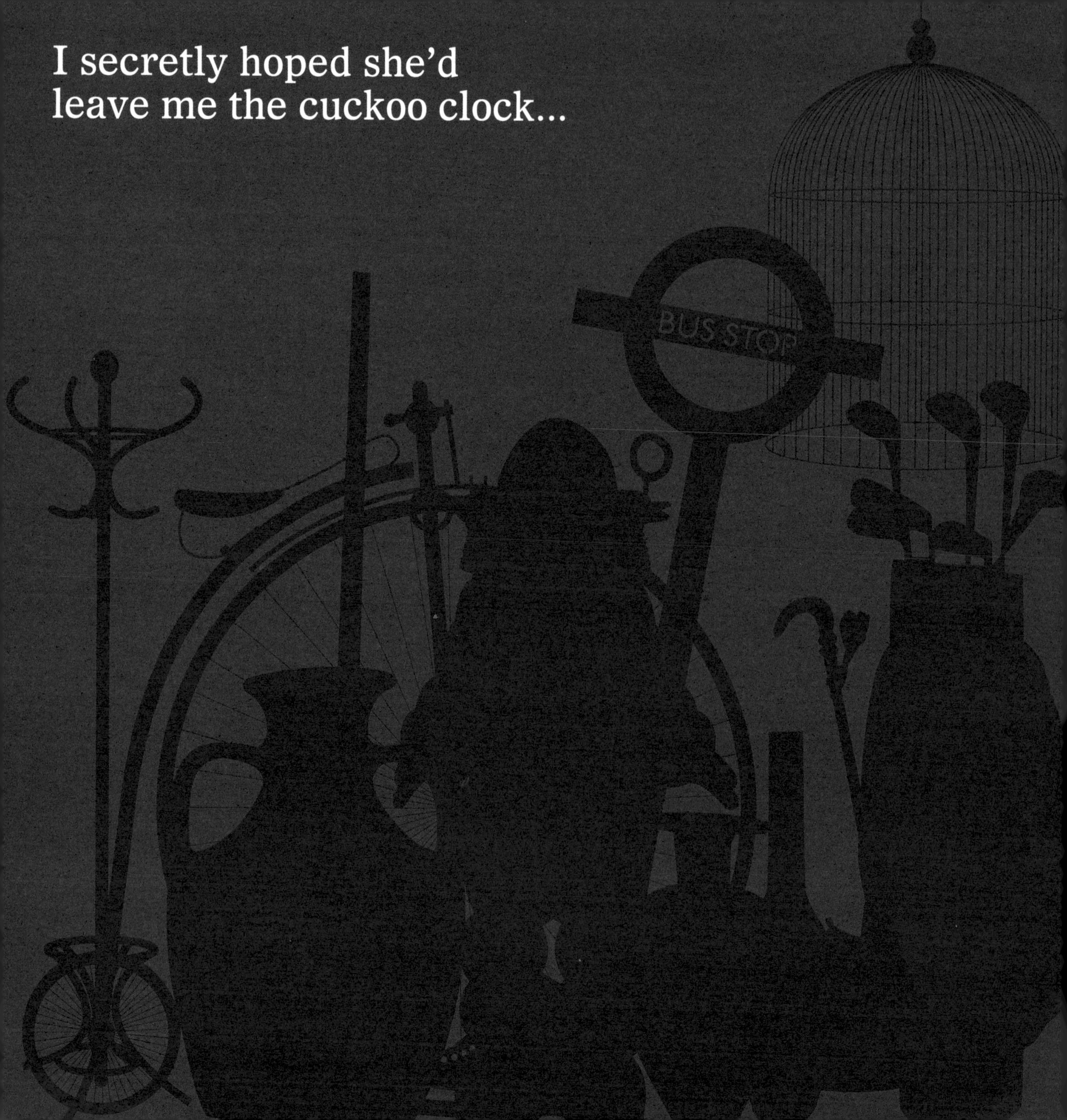

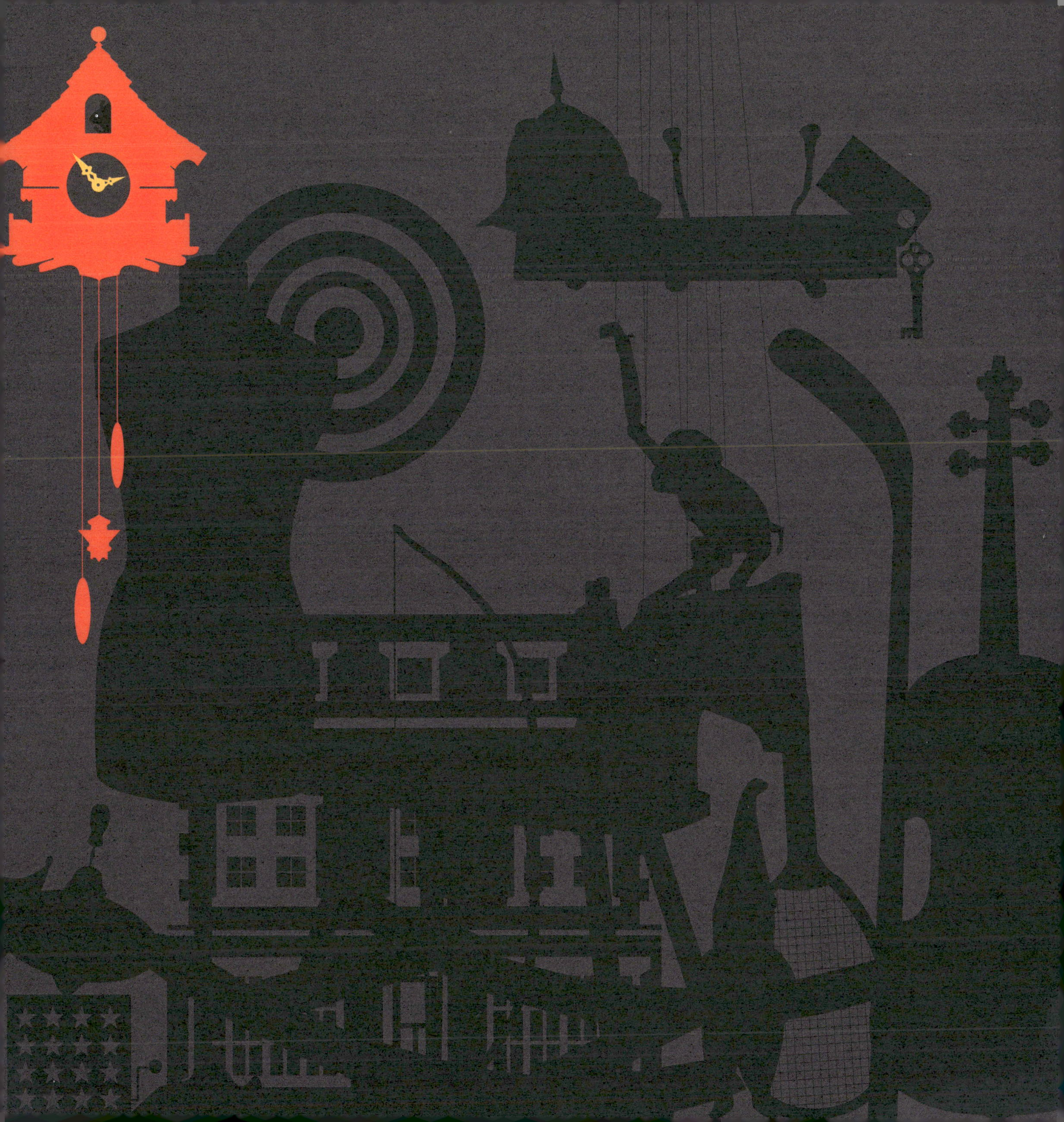

But she didn’t.
It was sent to her cousin
once-removed instead.

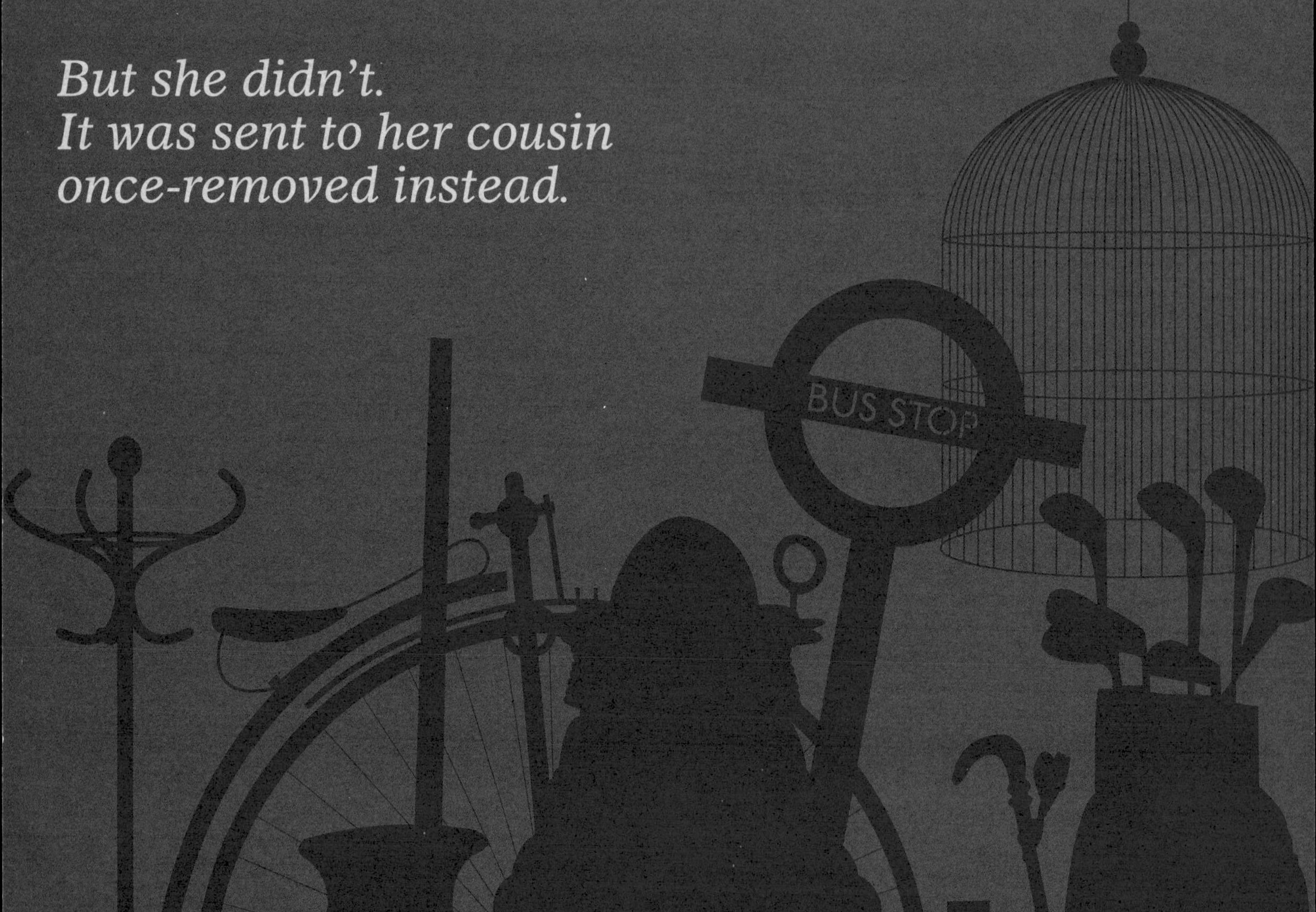

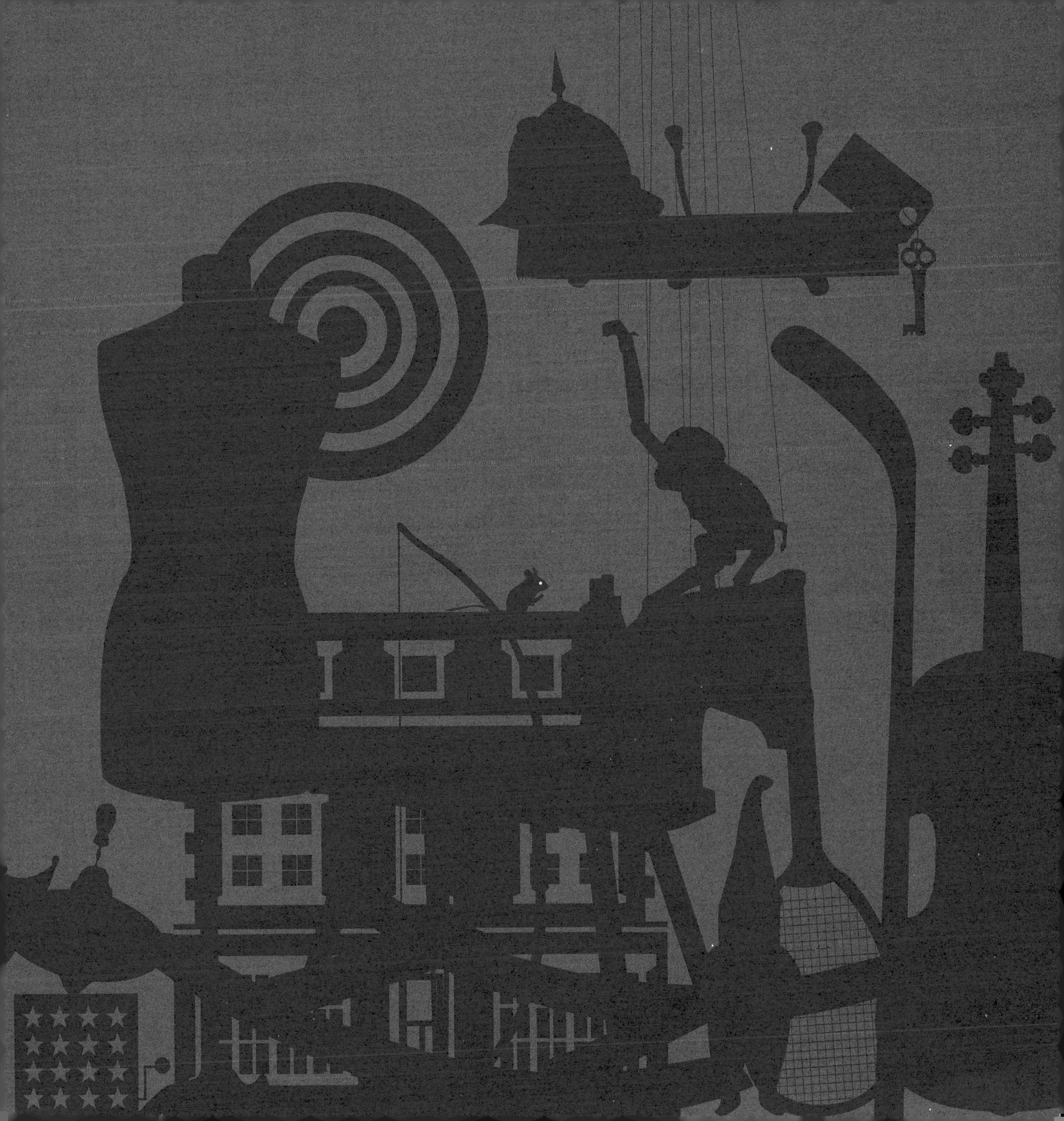

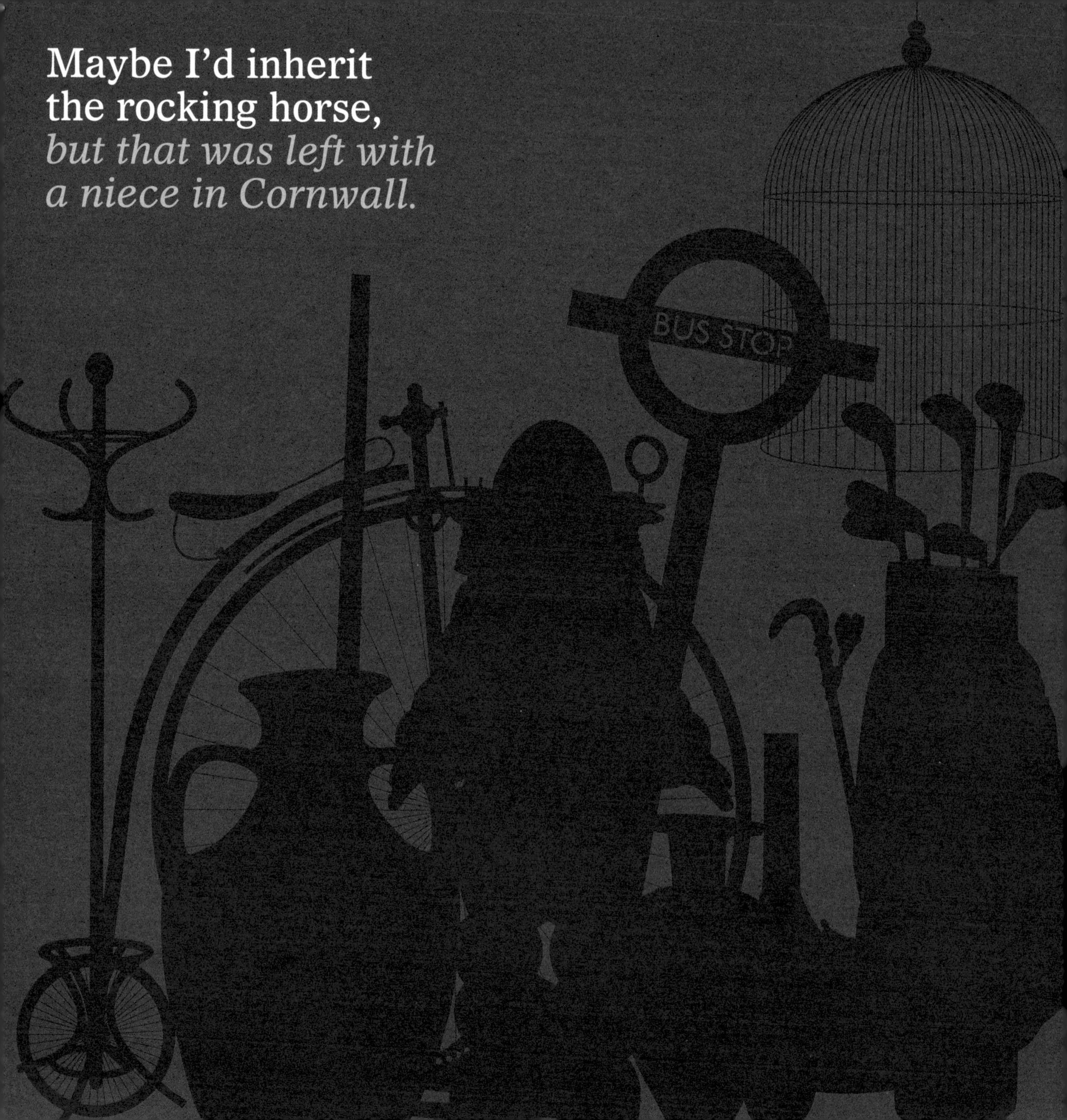
Maybe I'd inherit
the rocking horse,
*but that was left with
a niece in Cornwall.*
BUS STOP

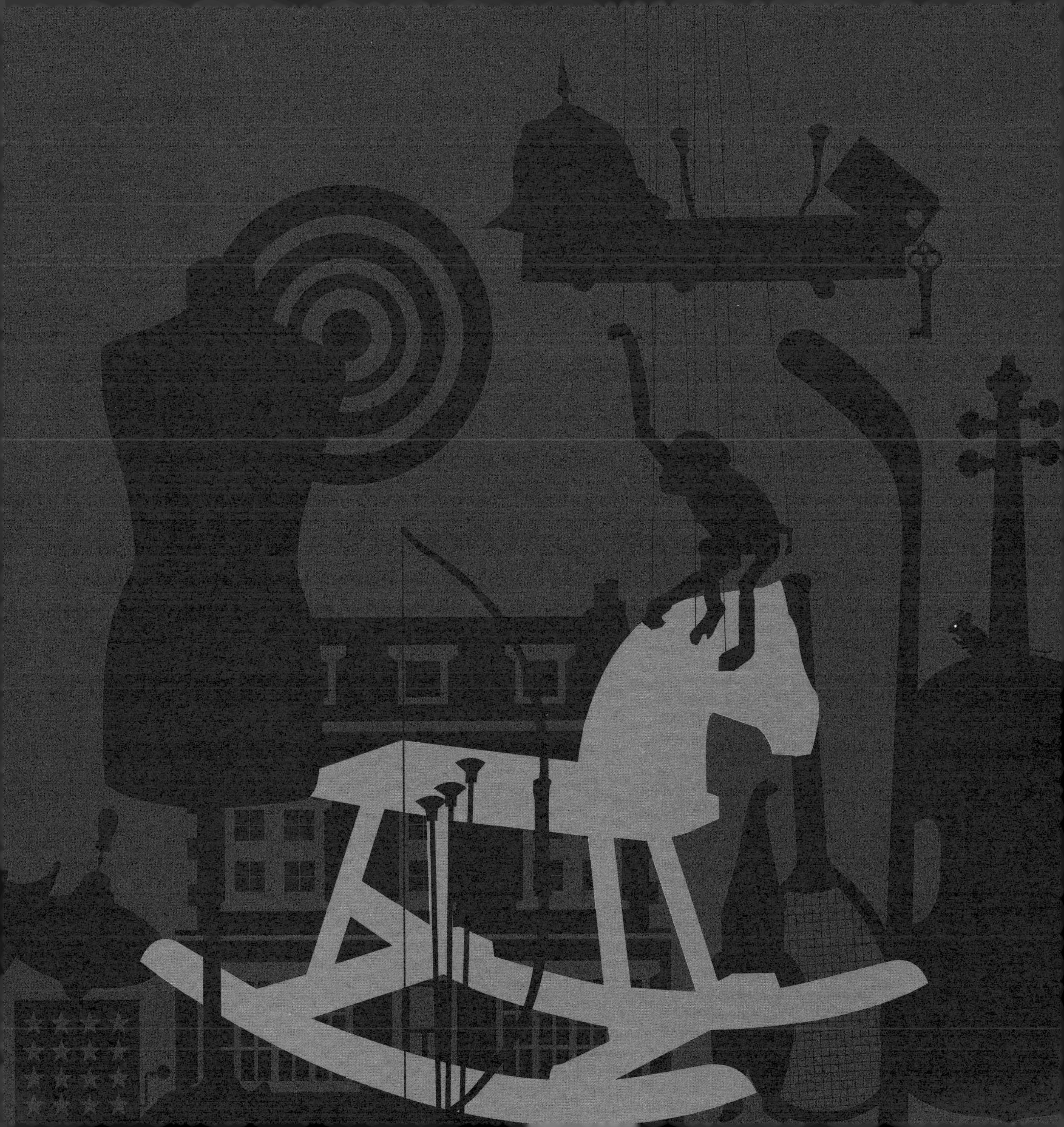

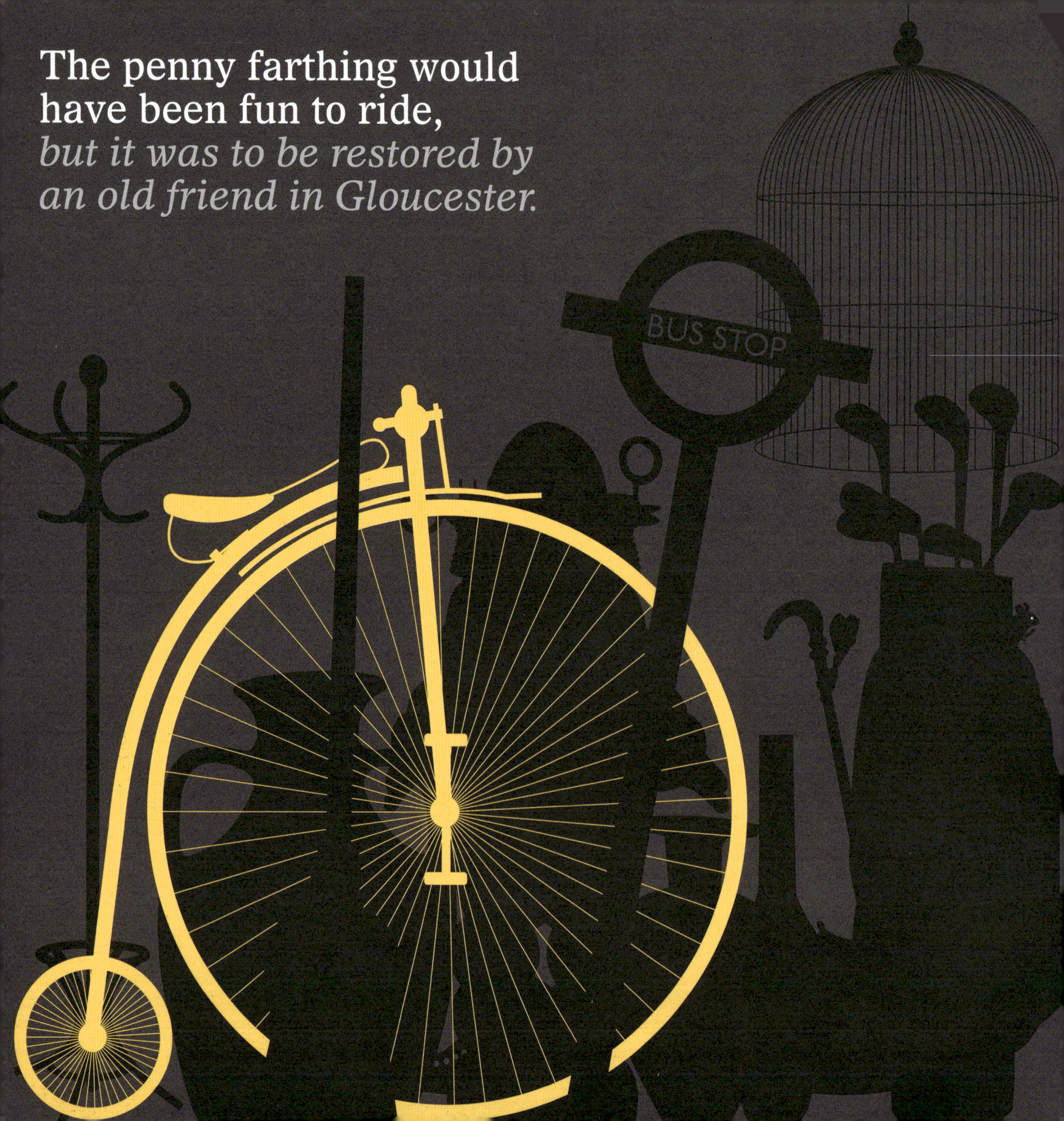

The penny farthing would have been fun to ride, *but it was to be restored by an old friend in Gloucester.*

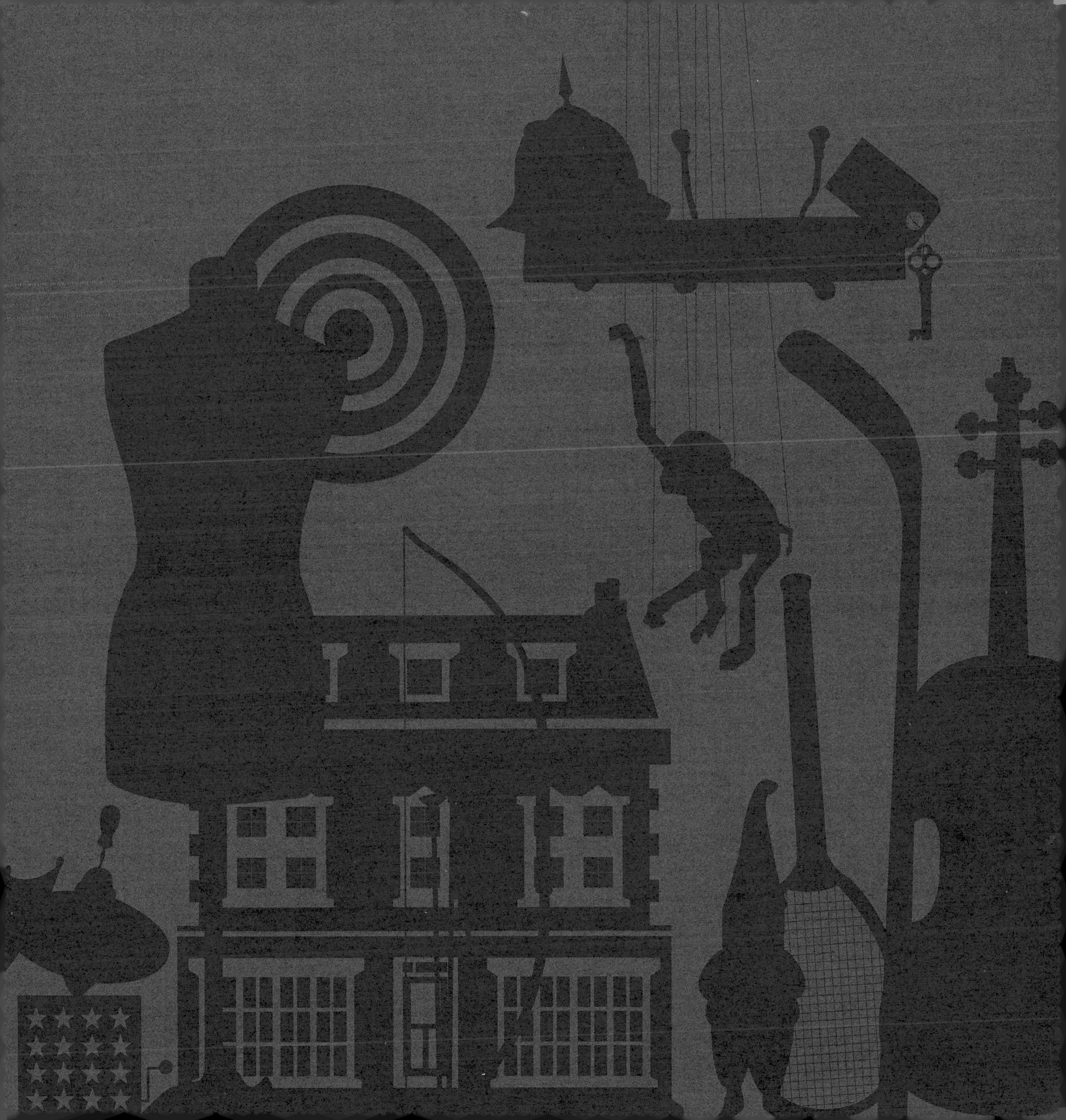

Perhaps I'd acquire
the golf clubs,
but these were left to
my brother, Thomas.

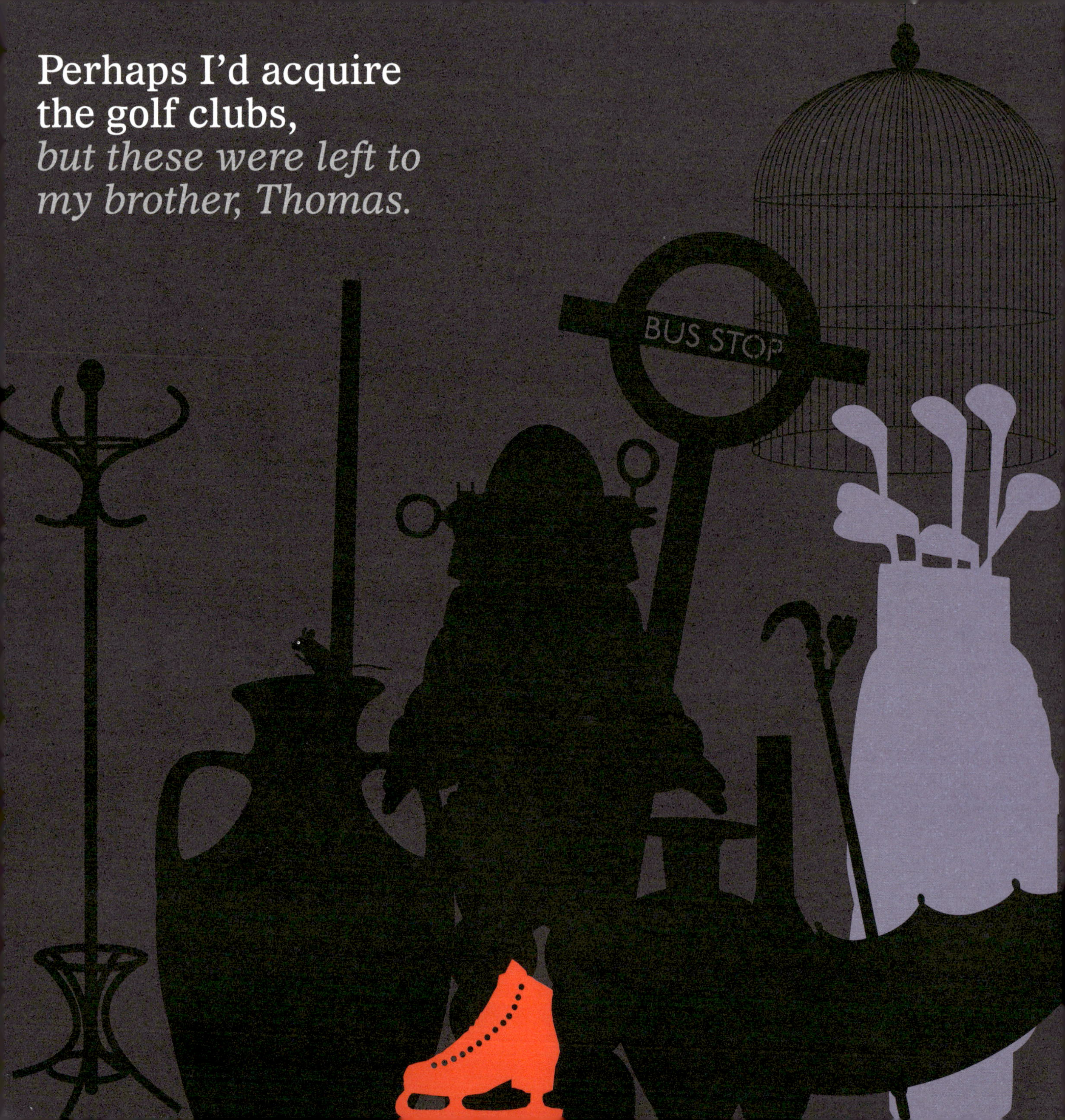

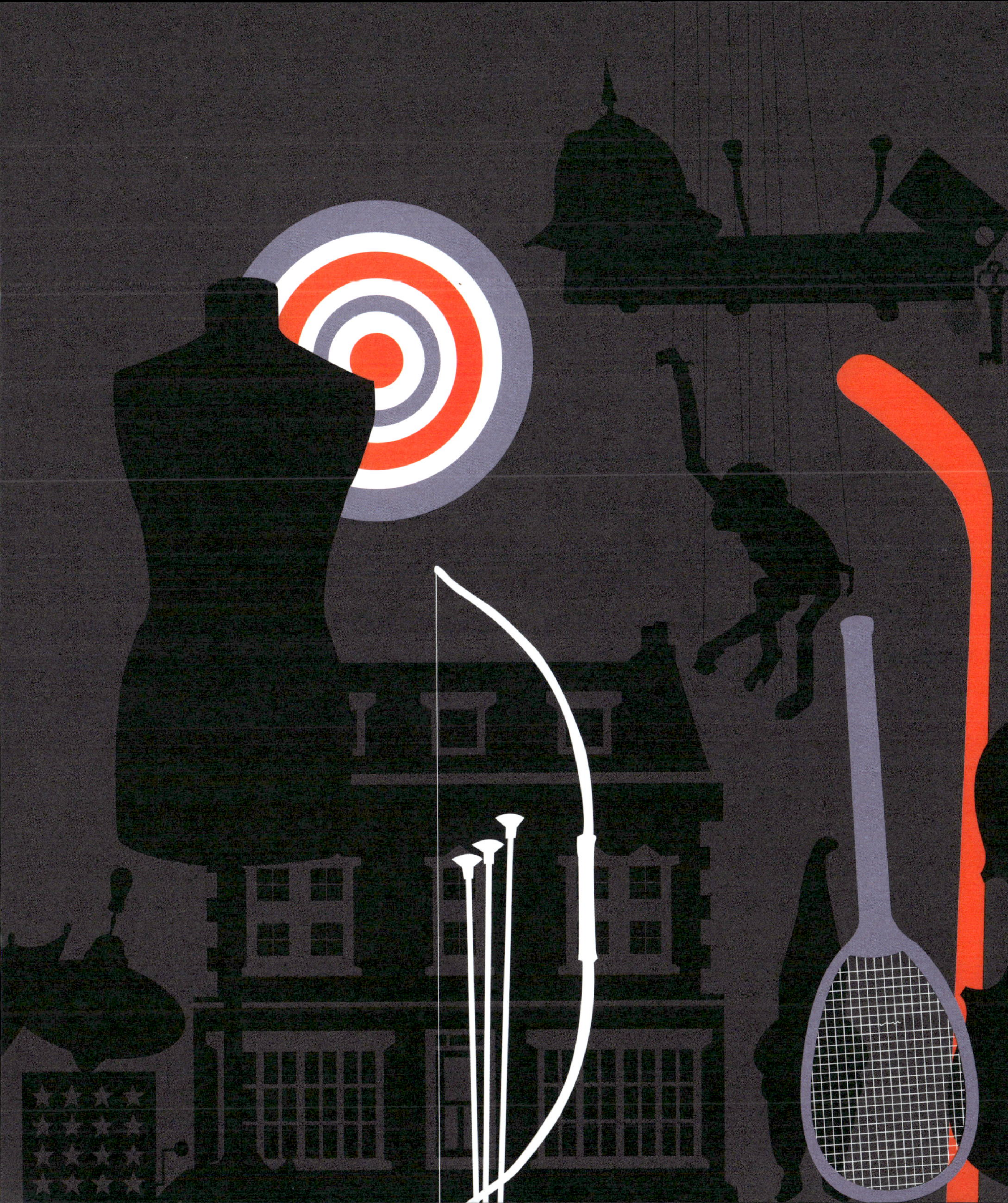

Maybe I'd be able
to learn the violin,
*but that made its way
to little Alfie next door.*

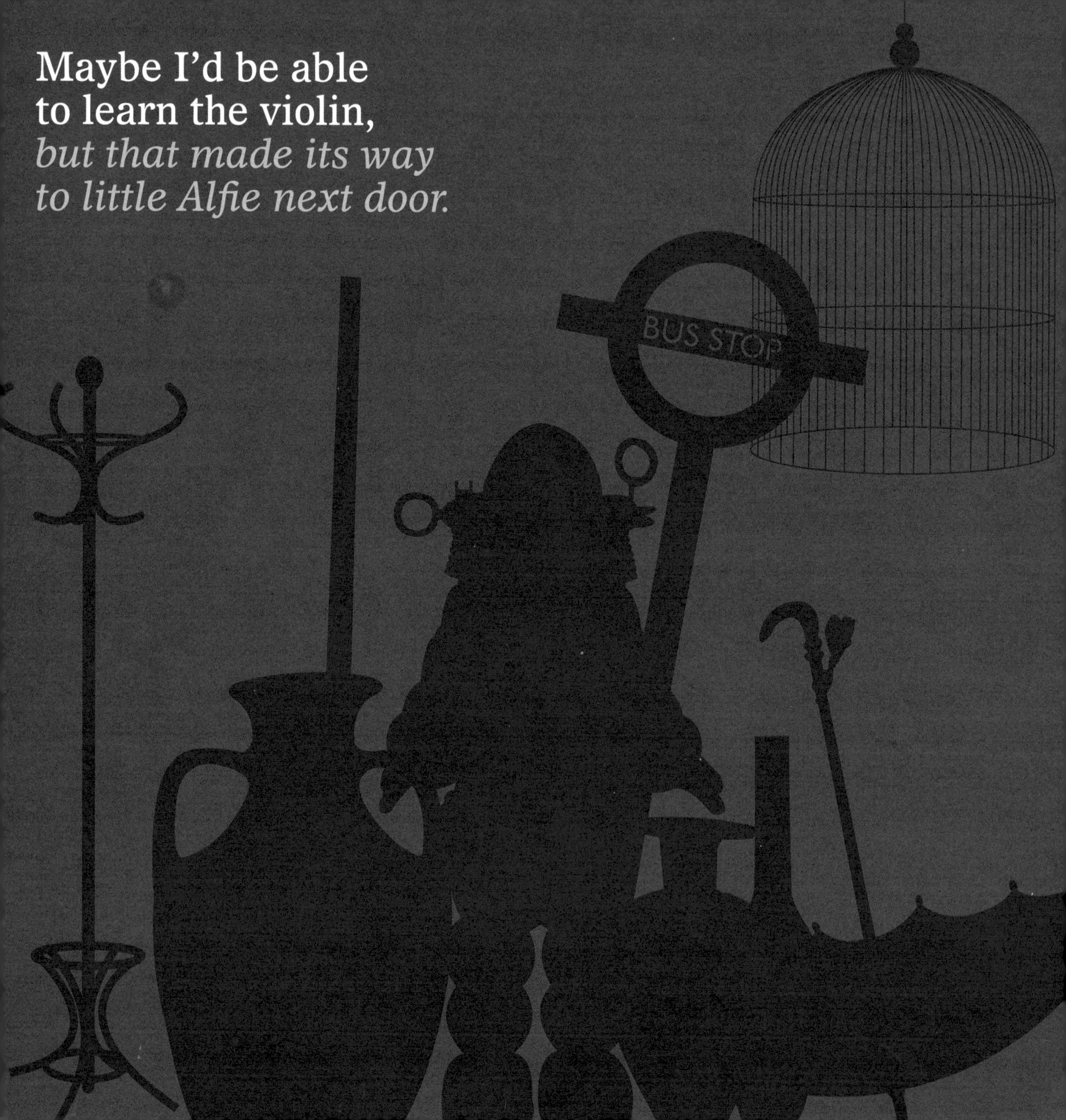

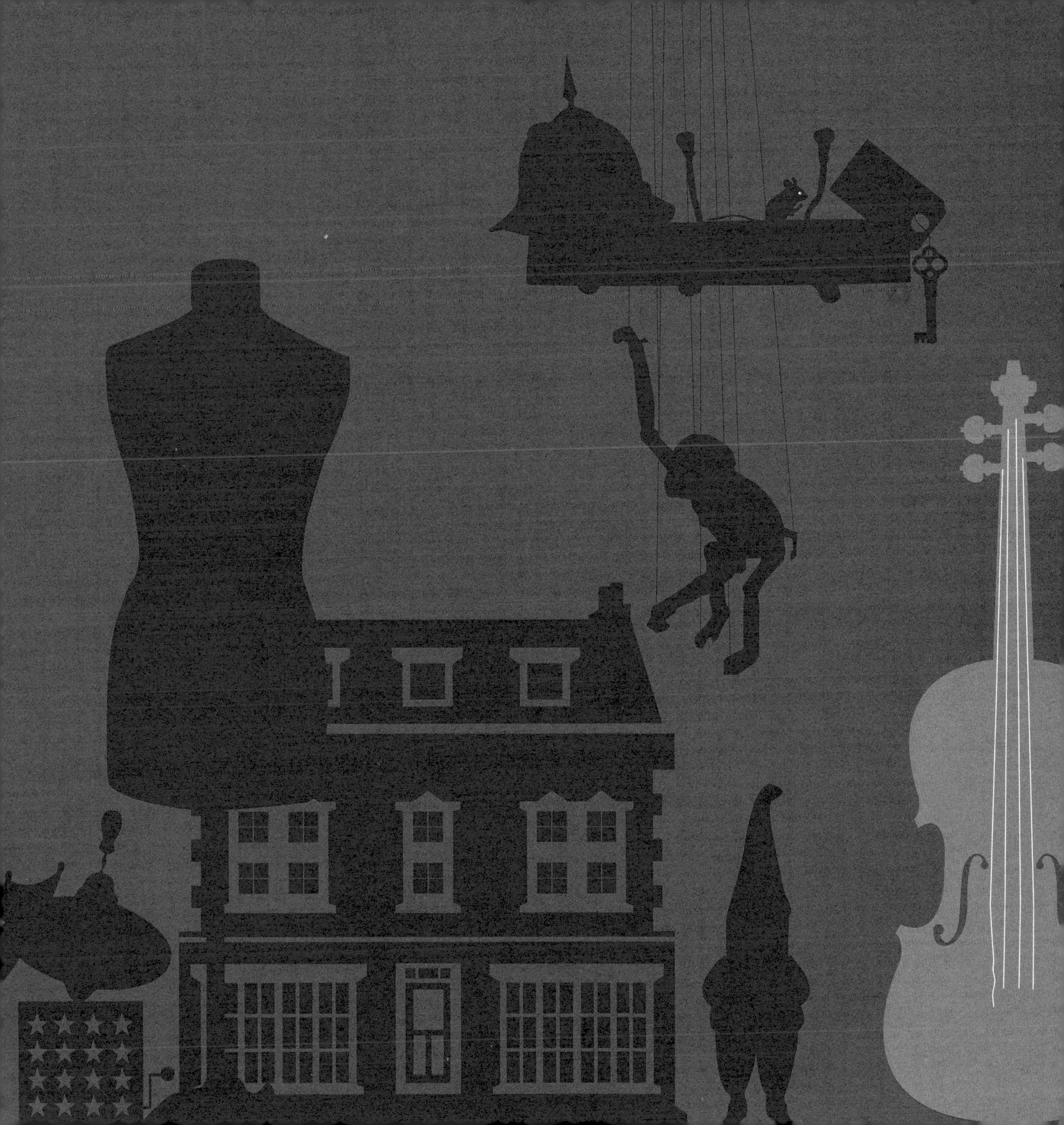

The fine collection of toys would have been a privilege to own, *but they were put on display at a London museum.*

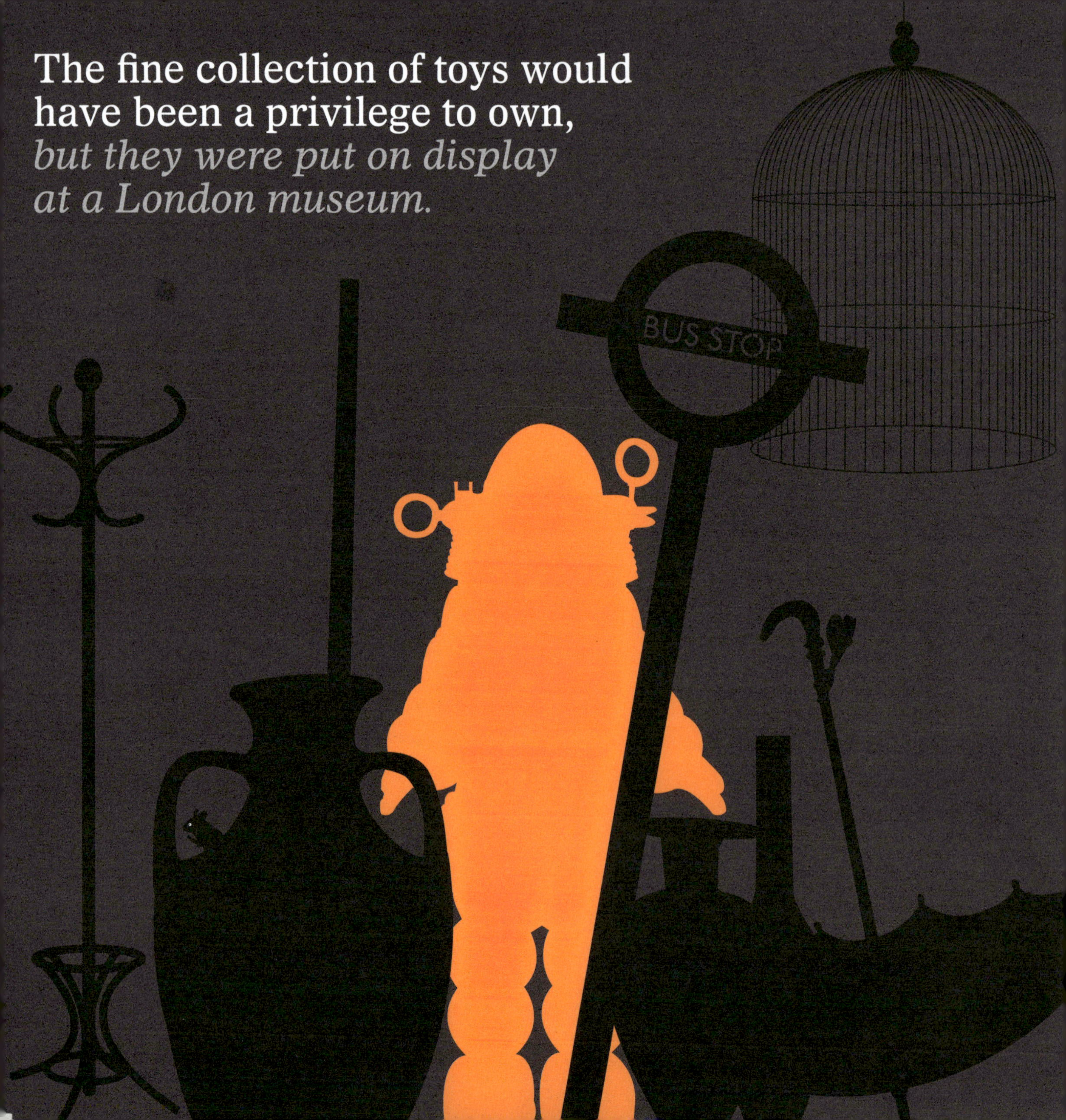

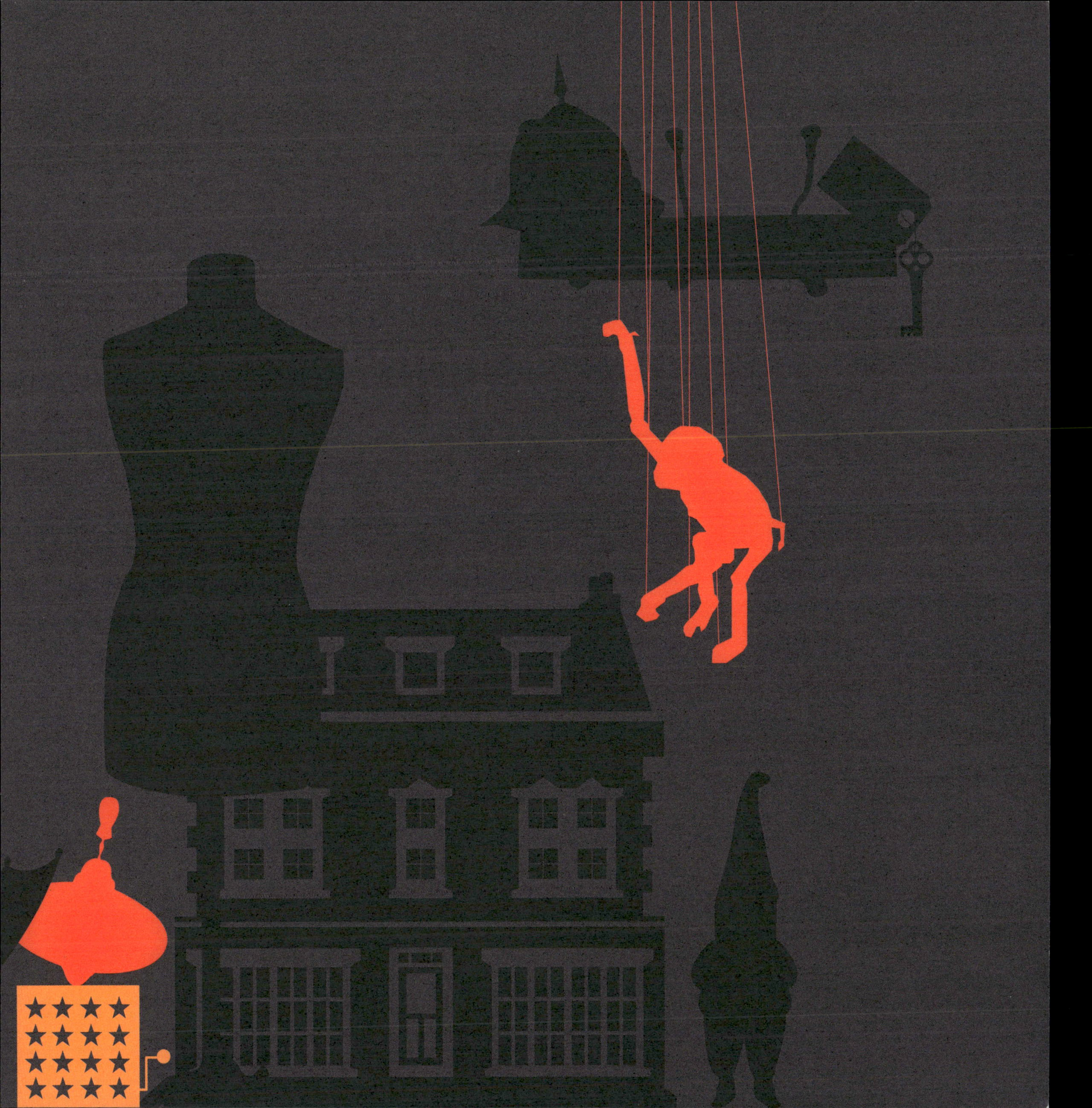

It would have been an honour to receive the splendid dollshouse, *but that was entrusted to Mable's sister, Marjorie.*

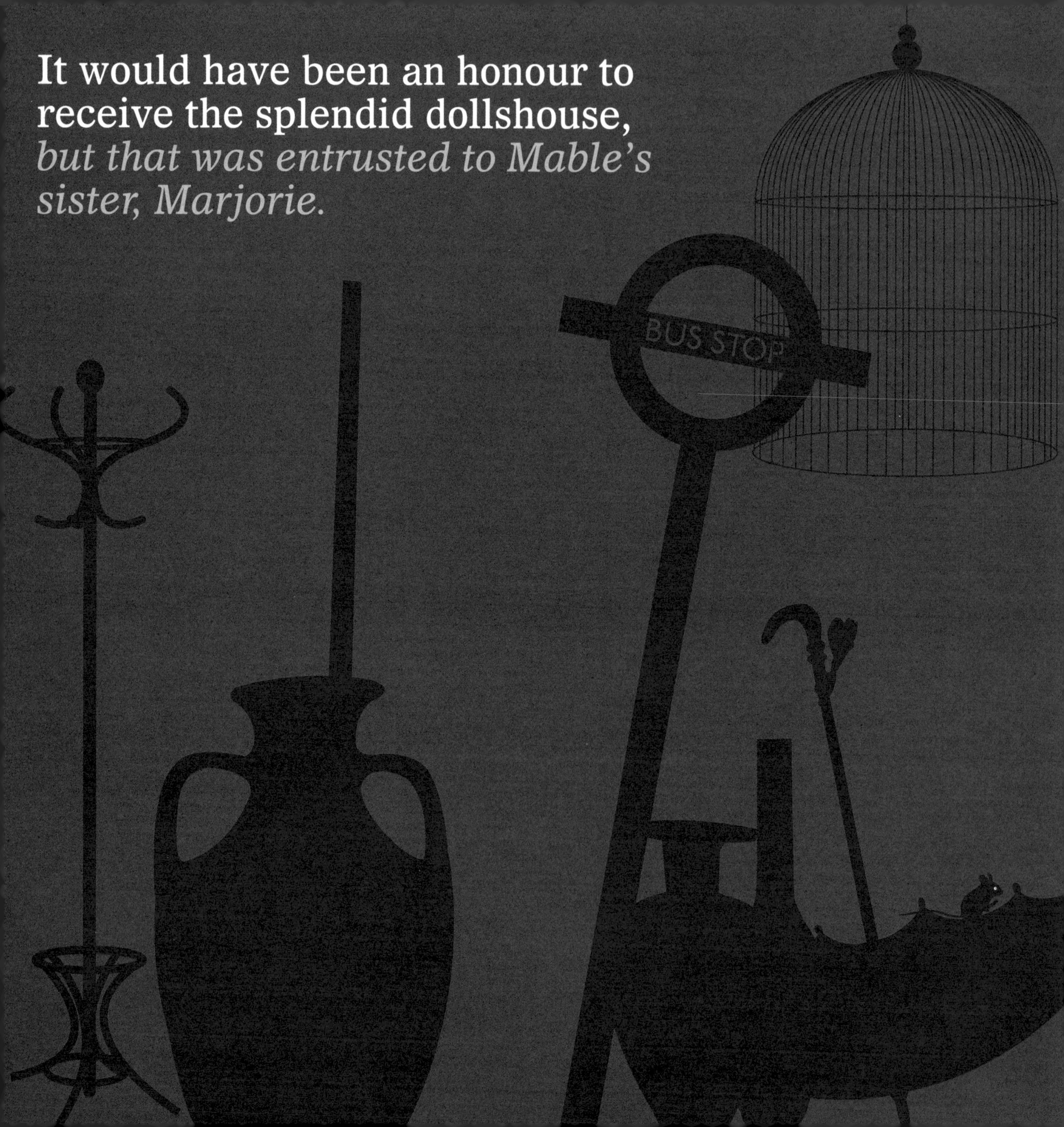

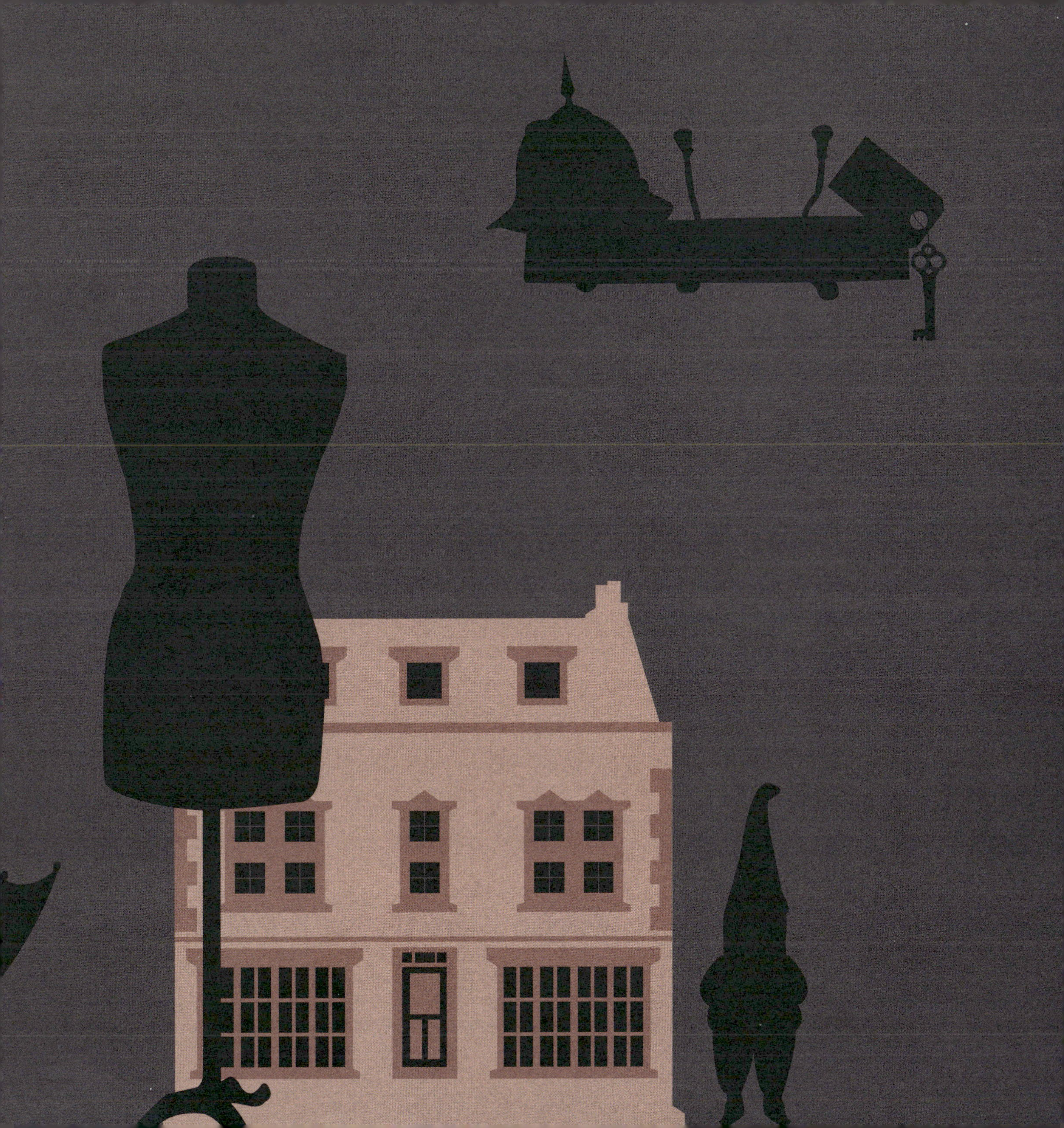

I could have found a good
home for her pottery,
*but it was carefully boxed and
dispatched to a family in St. Ives.*

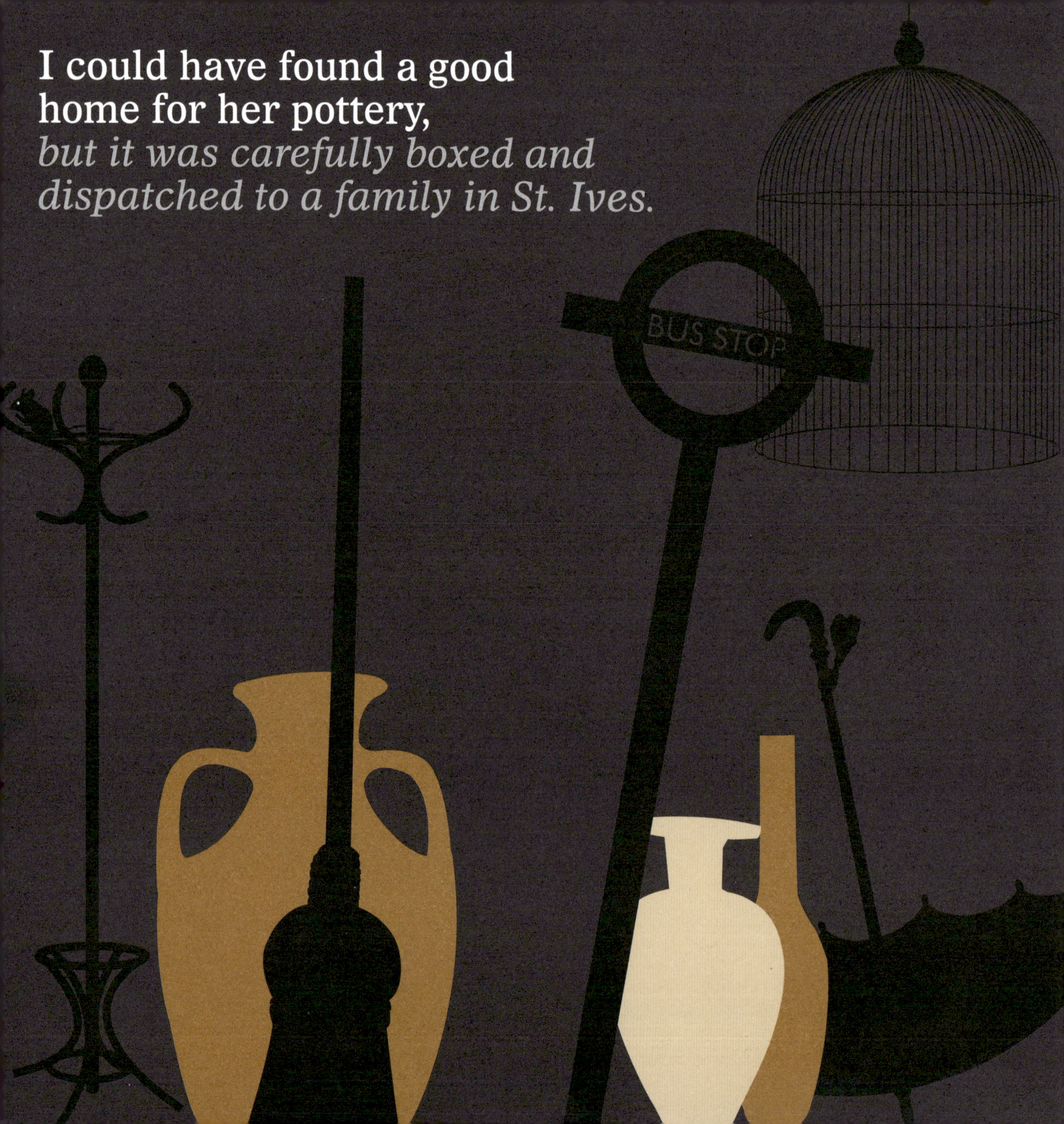

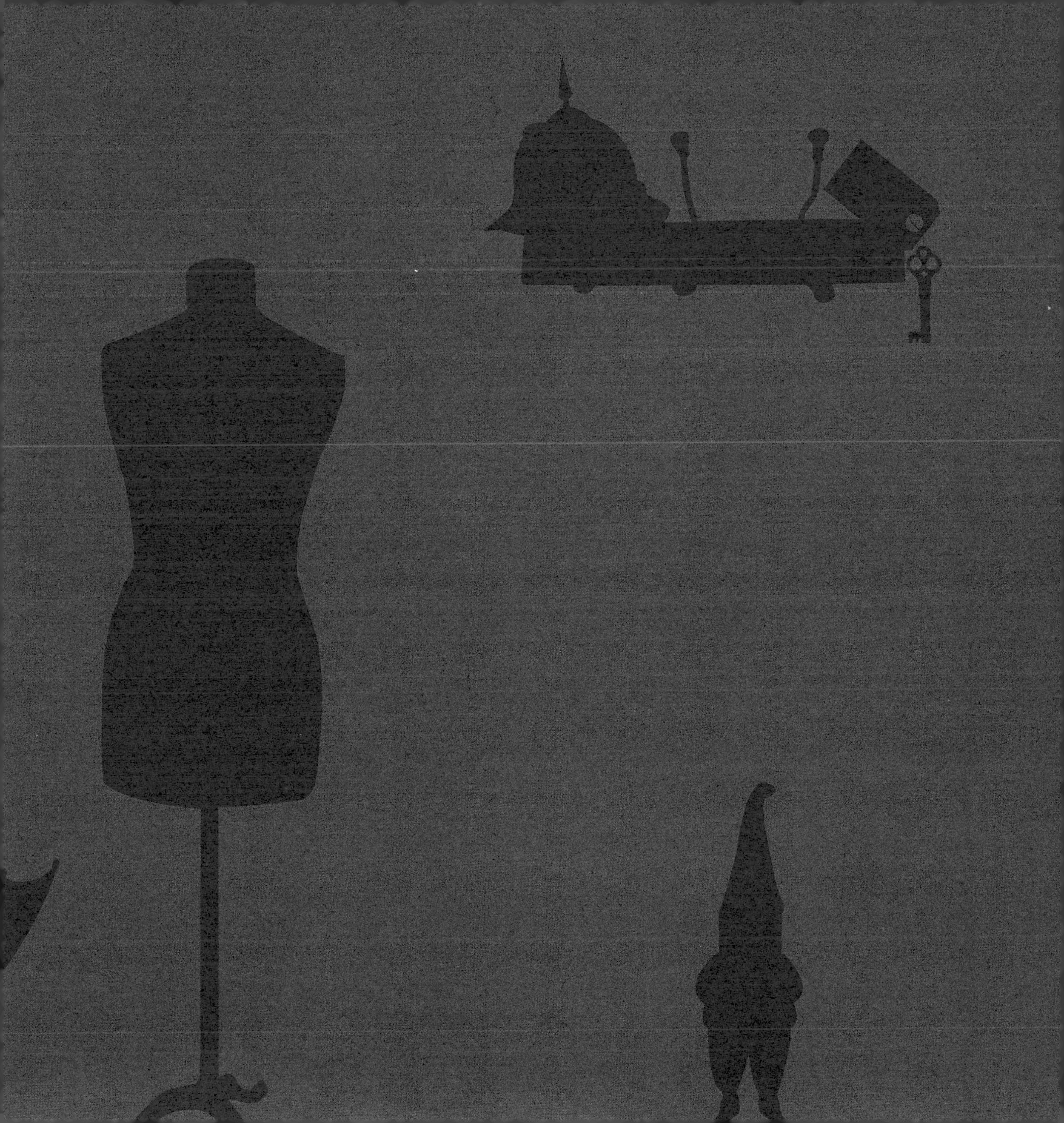

The garden gnome would have been a fond way to remember Mable, *but he made his way to a garden in Sussex.*

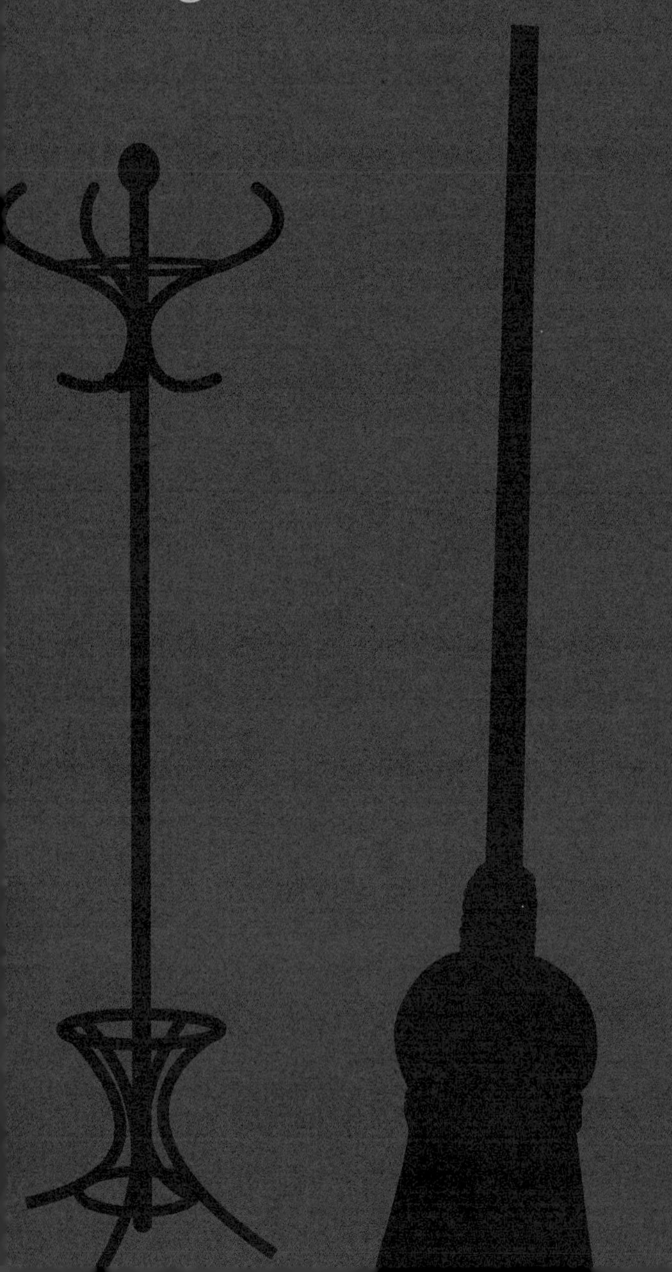

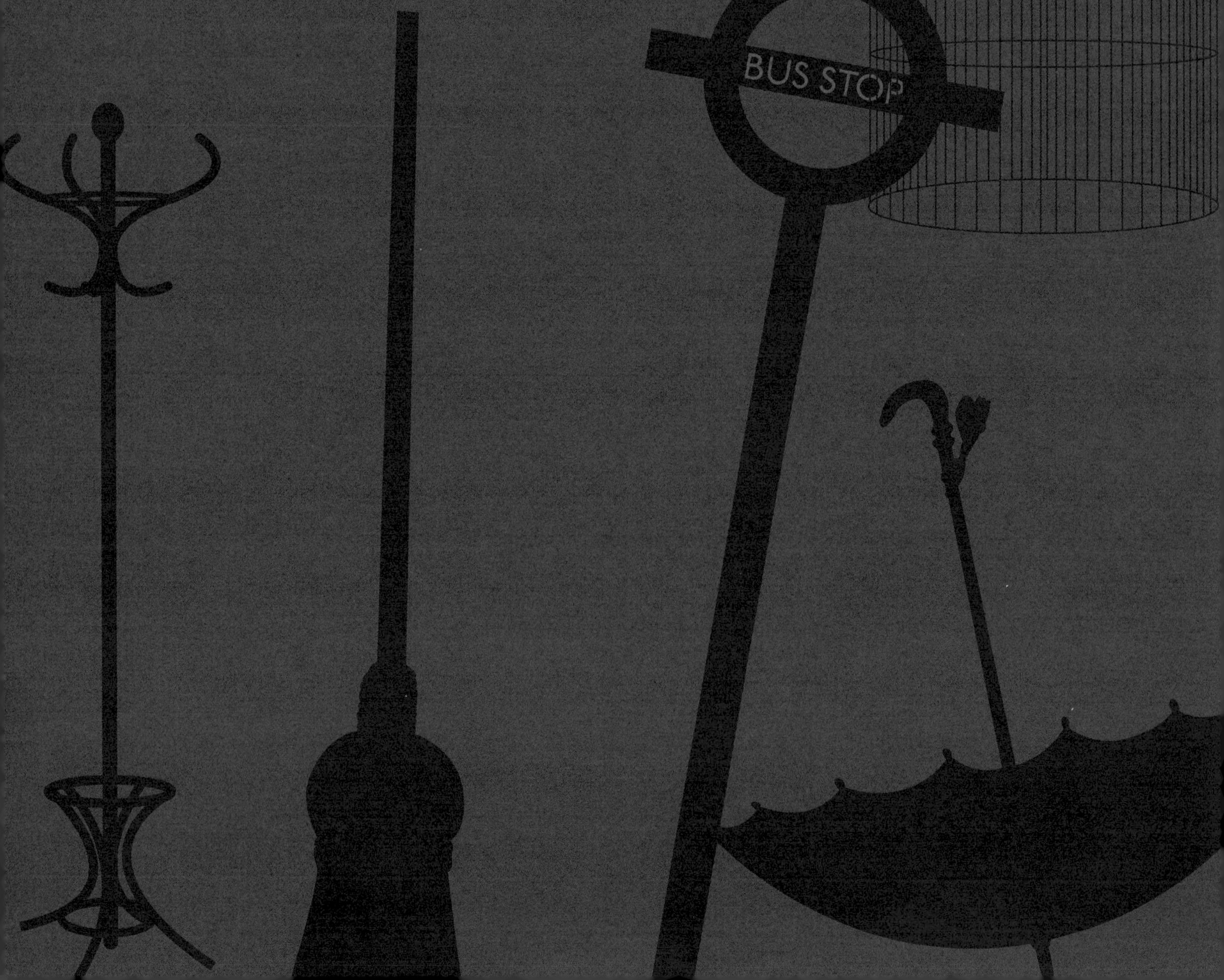

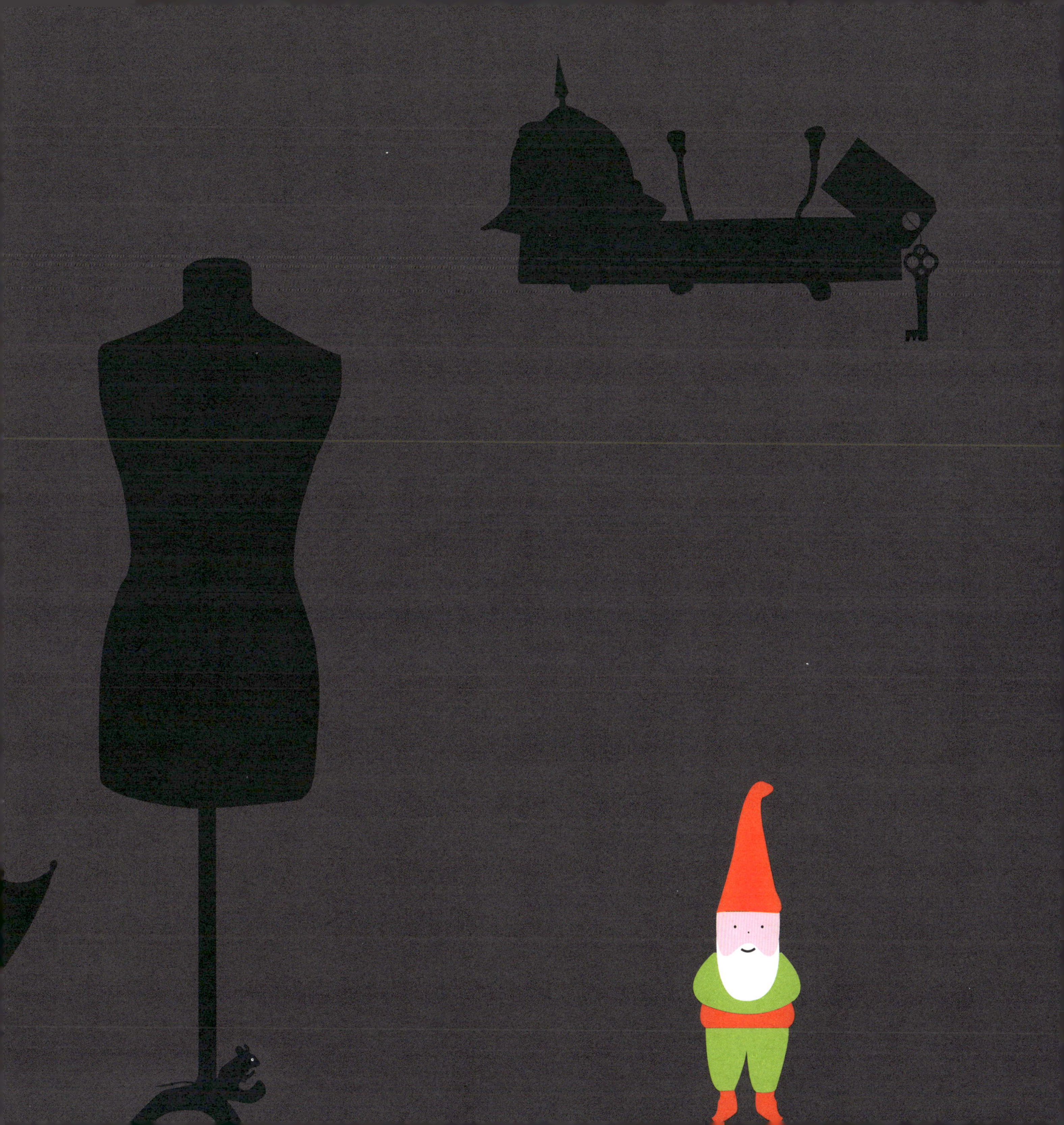

Even a tailor’s dummy or the umbrella would have come in useful, *but they were taken to the charity shop with everything else...*

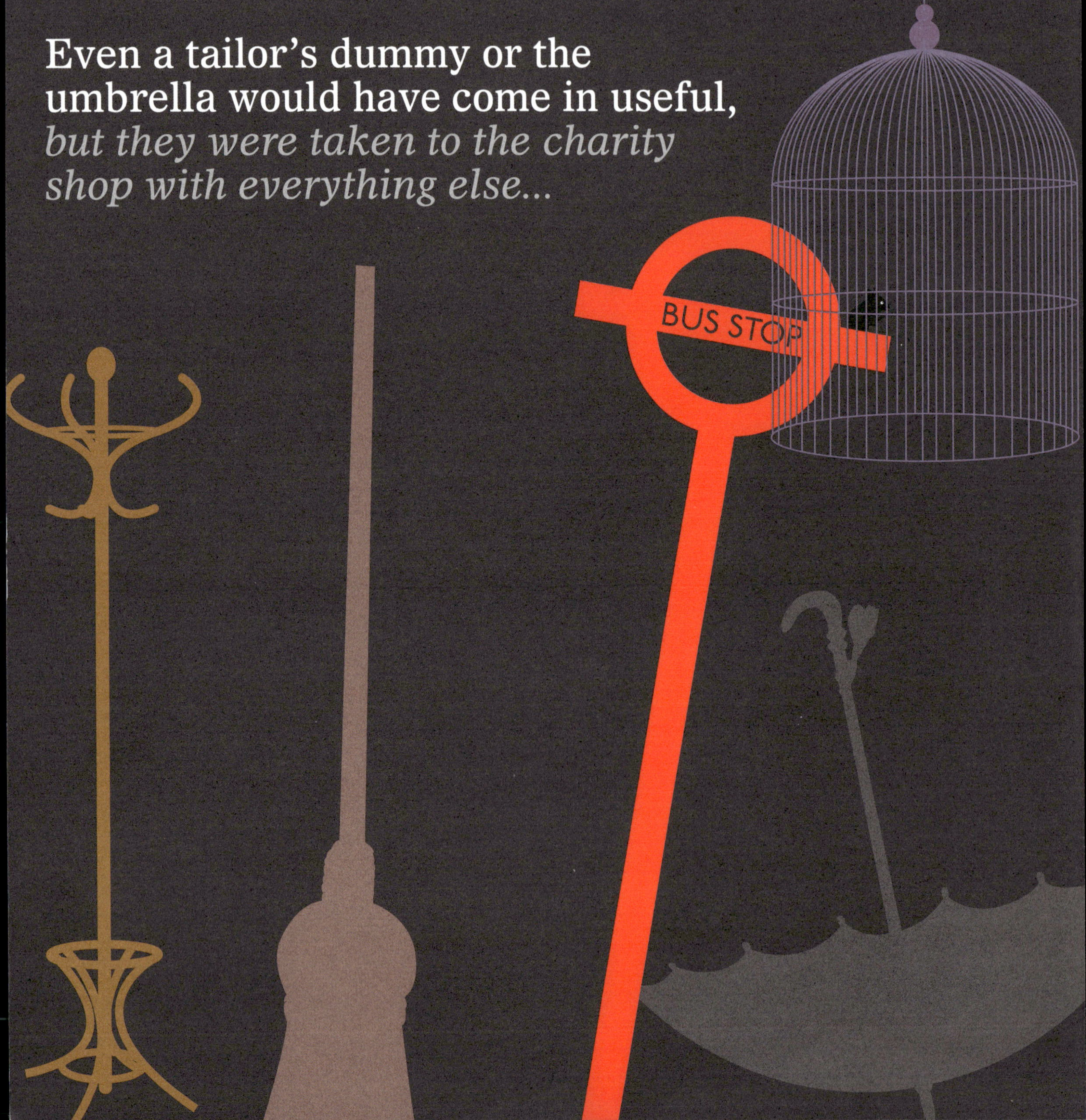

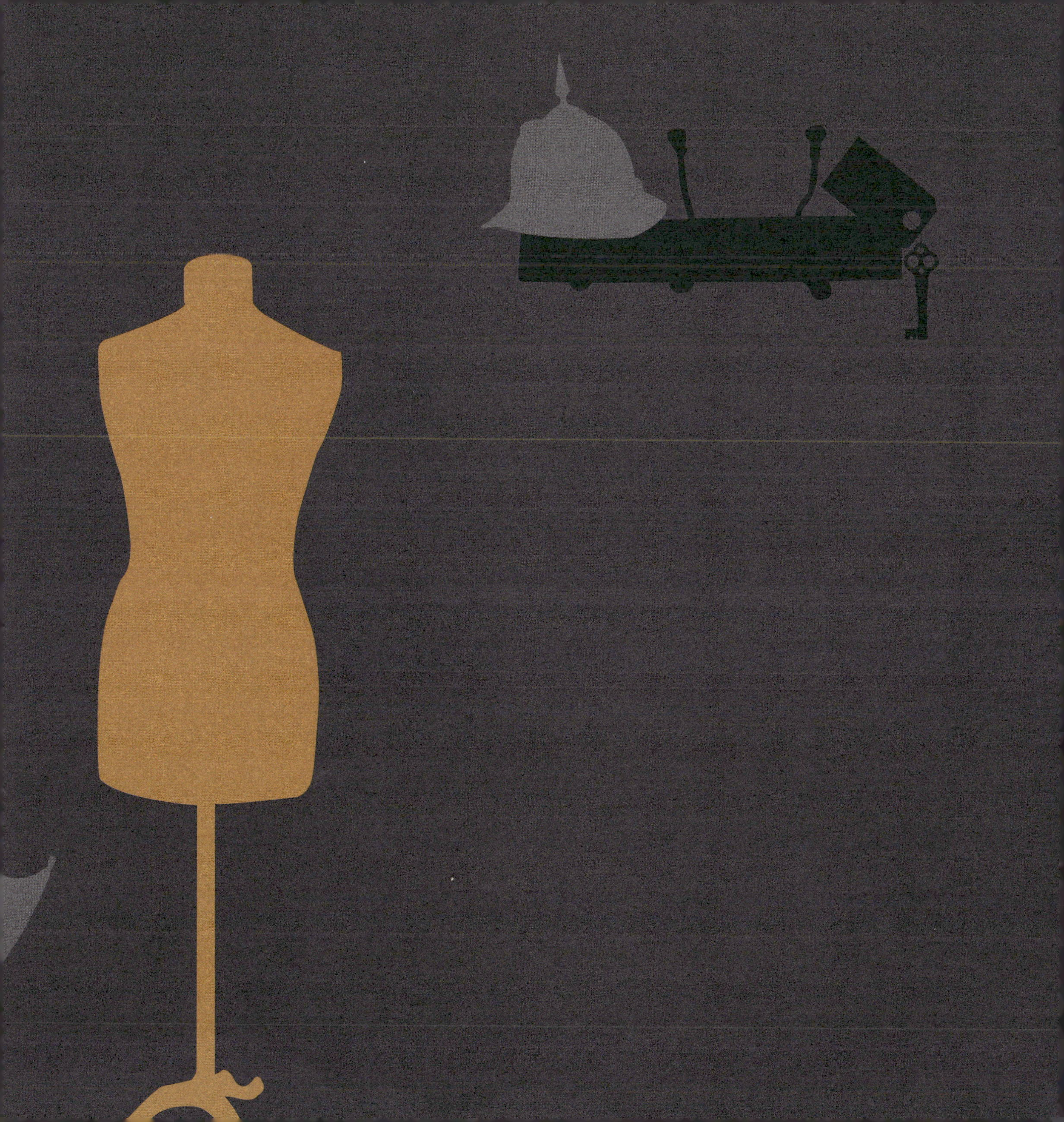

Everything, that is,
except for one thing...

Dear Nephew, here is the key to the house which is now yours.

I hope you fill it with as many treasures and memories as I did.

Love, Aunt Mable